Irish stories of loss and hope

EDITED BY DR. SUSAN DELANEY, THE IRISH HOSPICE FOUNDATION

THE IRISH HOSPICE FOUNDATION

ACKNOWLEDGEMENTS

Thank you to the writers, poets and artists who so generously shared their work and experiences, thus creating this anthology.

This project would not have been possible without the support of the Health Services Staffs Credit Union, and I am very grateful to them.

Thanks to Dublin City Council who contributed to the publishing costs of the project.

Thank you to Marguerite O Molloy, IMMA, for her help in sourcing and contacting the artists.

Thanks to Joe Woods and Deryn O Brien, Poetry Ireland, for helping to source poems and contacting the poets.

Thank you to Áine McCambridge who initially took on the administrative duties associated with this project, but contributed so much more through her ideas, enthusiasm and creativity.

Finally thank you to all the staff of IHF who helped bring this project to fruition, especially Caroline Lynch, Mary Millea and Ann-Marie Butler.

Dr. Susan Delaney
Bereavement Services Manager
Irish Hospice Foundation
April 2007

This book is dedicated to the memory of all whose stories are told within these pages. You have not been forgotten.

TABLE OF CONTENTS

PREFACE

THE MUSTARD SEED

A young woman who had lost her only son went from house to house clasping her dead child and pleading for medicine to bring him back to life. Finally, one man took pity on her and directed her to the Buddha telling her that he alone could help her. She found the Buddha high in the mountains and begged him for a cure.

"Yes there is a cure", he promised, "but I will need a handful of mustard seed from a house where no child, husband, parent or servant has died".

The young woman made the rounds of the local villages, looking for a house that had not been visited by death. At each house she encountered a different tale of loss. Slowly she came to realise that a house untouched by death did not exist. As dusk fell, she gently placed the body of her child in the forest and made her way back up to the Buddha.

"Did you obtain the mustard seed?" he asked.

"I did not" she replied. "The people of the village tell me, the living are few but the dead are many".

"You thought you alone had suffered a death", said the Buddha. "But the law of death states that among all living creatures there is no permanence". The Buddha directed her to cast her gaze back down the mountain, and to notice the flickering lights of the village; "We are all like the flame of those candles", he taught, "one moment lit, the next extinguished".

A TRADITIONAL BUDDHIST TEACHING ON DEATH

Brendan Kennelly

I SEE YOU DANCING FATHER

No sooner downstairs after the night's rest
And in the door
Than you started to dance a step
In the middle of the kitchen floor.

And as you danced
You whistled.
You made your own music
Always in tune with yourself.

Well, nearly always, anyway.
You're buried now
In Lislaughtin Abbey
And whenever I think of you

I go back beyond the old man
Mind and body broken
To find the unbroken man.
It is the moment before the dance begins,

Your lips are enjoying themselves
Whistling an air.
Whatever happens or cannot happen
In the time I have to spare
I see you dancing, father.

Reprinted by kind permission of the Poet
From BBC '*The Nations's Favourite Poems of Remembrance*'

REMEMBERING MY MOTHER

There is a farmer's market in Ranelagh, in Dublin, which operates every Sunday in the grounds of a local school. I go there all the time now, because since my mother died on December 16, 2004, I no longer spend every weekend in Derry looking after her, which I did for four years.

I go to the market to buy pickled herring. It is delicious. It was one of my favourite foods in childhood. A man used to come round the streets every week in the nineteen forties and fifties, wheeling a barrel of herring on a handcart, and I would go with my mother to buy some. The dead, silvered fish, floating to the brim in brine, were a source of wonder. The smell was heady. The wooden barrel itself was magnificent, as were the broad iron bands which held it together: it was a work of art. I wonder if that's where the word "artisan" comes from?

My mother just loved buying those herring. She loved the sight, smell and taste of them. They were cheap to buy, which added to her pleasure. My father also adored this meal - herring with boiled potatoes.

I loved the story my mother often told when he settled down to this great dinner. When my father was a newly married young man, his friend Mickey Quigley asked him to embark on a joint investment in a barrel of herring. My cautious father declined the offer and stayed in the civil service, on a reasonable, steady wage, which was a big thing in the Bogside, where the male unemployment rate in the Bogside averaged fifty per cent.

Mickey went on to become Derry's premier fishmonger, and comfortably off with it. My mother used to tease my father that she should have married Mickey, who was best man at her wedding and had asked her to marry him the night before she married my father. Even after she married my father, and though he was happily married himself, Mickey sent my mother red roses on her birthday, right up until he died. It was a running joke between the three of them, my mother, my father, and Mickey. The herring and the roses were a great story in our family. My mother always ended the telling of it by saying "Ah, sure, I was right to marry your father."

My mother outlived my father and Mickey. They are all gone now, as is the tradition of selling herring in the street.

So my heart leaped with memory a few months after she died, when I stumbled on the feast of pickled herring in the farmer's market in Ranelagh, in Dublin. I felt the sorrow of my mother's death physically lift off me. She was joyfully present to me that day. I enjoyed a lovely dinner of herring and potatoes.

A few hours later, the sorrow came crashing back like a tidal wave. Why, oh Jesus, why, hadn't I tried to buy pickled herring for my mother in the last years of her life, when she could not walk, couldn't go out the town to shop, and relied on people like me to do the shopping for her?

Why hadn't I searched Derry, Dublin, the Internet, for pickled herring? Why hadn't I asked a Swedish friend of mine, who comes on regular visits to Ireland, to bring over the picked herring on which that country royally dines?

The sadness of that - that lack of imagination on my part about how to please my disabled mother - lacerated me. I had spent years devising ways and means to please her, often successfully, but I had not thought of that simple thing: pickled herring.

On the other hand, she never thought to ask for it. There I go again, trying to excuse myself.

The laceration has eased. My mother is two years dead now. I can buy the pickled herring and think of her and the glad way we all were, once, a long time ago. I accept the flash of sadness that comes with the meal and then I welcome the joy that the pickled herrings bring. They bring my mother straight back into my life.

I have been ambushed and consoled in many such small ways since she died. All consolation is welcome. The feast of pickled herring has become a ritual. ▨

■ NELL MC CAFFERTY'S AUTOBIOGRAPHY "NELL" IS AVAILABLE IN BOOKSHOPS

OUR MOTHERS DIE ON DAYS LIKE THIS

When there isn't a puff
and the walk from the bus stop
to the front door
isn't worth the longed-for
out-of-the question cup of sweet tea
she can never have
because doctor do-little-or nothing
told her face to face
it was the sugar or the clay
the choice was hers.

The choice was no choice
he knew it, she knew it.

When the heavy bill on the hall floor
with the final notice reminded her
once and for all she must turn out the lights,
her Angelus bell rang and rang.

Reprinted by kind permission of the Poet

From *'An Awful Racket'* published by Bloxdale Books

NO MORE DADDY'S GIRL

The phone rang at 5 one morning. I woke up and got out of bed, feeling disorientated. It was my brother. I remember wondering what on earth he was phoning me for at that hour of the morning, and then he said it: "*I'm afraid Dad is dead*". I stood, silent, still. Then I spoke very forcefully, "*not my Dad!*" I willed it not to be true. Then I heard my husband groan behind me, and I knew that it was real. My father was dead, and I was not longer Daddy's little girl. I sat down and wept. I wept for the loss of my father, the one man in my life who had always loved me unconditionally. I wished I had not picked up the phone. If I hadn't answered it, he would still be alive, at least to me.

I drove to my Mother's house alone. I had to go immediately, and I had to go alone. I couldn't wait for my husband or my children. Actually I didn't want them with me. I didn't want to have to deal with their feelings. At that moment there was no room in me to give thought to their pain, my own was so overwhelming.

When I saw my mother, my heart just broke; I felt it crack. I knew something had utterly changed inside me forever.

I wanted to see my father. He was in the living room. He had died in his comfortable chair, with his feet up on a footstool, a glass of whiskey at one hand, and the ashtray in the other. I am glad I saw him as he was, because it made me truly see that my father was gone. It comforted me to see how peaceful he looked.

Then the funeral car arrived. The men who came into our house were calm, big, dark presences. They seemed to know what to do, so we just let them take my father out the front door and put him in the back of the black car. That was unbearable. We just stood and allowed him to go. I thought there would be some sort of sign, but they just drove away.

I don't know how I got through the funeral. Afterwards there was the drive to the grave, a strange, surreal experience. My mother and I kept talking about how lovely the service was. It didn't seem real.

The burial was very difficult for me. It was a cold day, and I did not want to see my father lowered into the ground. My mother looked tiny, perished and frail, and I left the graveyard as quickly as I could.

Looking back, I feel everything was too rushed. I wish we had waked my father in the house, because he was a countryman, and it would have been fitting. But we left all the details to the funeral director, because none of us were capable of making decisions at the time. I remember feeling that we were very much alone in our loss, even though the family spent days together in the house. We talked and comforted each other as best we could, but each of us was in our own hell. My older brother had to make all kinds of decisions such as dealing with the finances. My younger brother had to fly in from England to find his father dead in a funeral home.

I got through the next few days with help from friends and family. People called to the house and offered words of comfort. Many of them did not know what to say, but I really appreciated their coming. Now I understand the importance of the small gesture, the practical gifts and the kind word.

During the first six months after my father's death, I went to my mother's house for breakfast everyday. This was a small, but important, thing. I know it helped her to get past that gut-wrenching lonely feeling she had on awakening each morning to the knowledge that her husband was dead. Being in one another's company helped both of us to get through those first shattering months.

Over time the intensity of my grief has eased. At the beginning I would wake at night, weeping. I missed my father so much. My heart jumped when I caught sight of an older man walking ahead of me on the road, wearing a trench coat so like my father's. I wanted to stop him and talk to him.

One morning, 6 months after Dad died, I found a letter he had written to me when I lived in America. It was a fantastic, terrible gift. I read it over and over, and found myself crying at intervals throughout the whole day.

My father's death changed me in ways I could never have imagined. There are days now when I do not think of him, and other days when I am overwhelmed with sadness that he is not here to share our lives. I have learned that life is precious and can be taken from you suddenly, without warning. Because I know this, I celebrate the very act of being alive. I choose to enjoy the many gifts that life has given me-now-at this very moment. I say the things I want to say to those I love. I grasp the opportunities that come my way and face whatever challenges each particular day brings. I am thankful to be alive. ▣

COT

We cringed around your bed in the hospital ward.
The matron announced you would die in half an hour.
She spoke as if dictating from a timetable.
Always in Italy the trains run on time.
I was dispatched to telephone the relations
But visitors to the dying had access only to a payphone.
None of the family had any change.
I had to borrow two tenpenny pieces
From the matron who had scheduled your death.
The first payphone did not work but the second did.
The relations said they would be with us in no time.
When I came scuttling back into the ward
And peered over the shoulders of my brothers and sisters
I saw that the deathbed had become a cot
And that you, Daddy, were a small, agèd infant
Struggling to stay alive in the world.
You were kicking up your legs in the air,
Brandishing your bony white knuckles.
I realised that you were my newborn son.
What kind of a son will you be to me?
Will you be as faithful a son to me
As you have been a father?
As intimate, as funny, as alien?
As furry, as skinny, as flighty?

Old man, infant boy,

As you writhe there

On your backside

In your cot

How helpless you are,

A minuscule helplessness

Heaving with innocence;

A baby dinosaur

With an expiry date.

You begin to bawl.

My mother takes off her black glove

And lays her hand

Across your threadbare skull.

You wave her goodbye,

She who loves you

After one day

And forty-four years.

You go back to sleep,

The black world to rue.

Bonny boys are few.

Don't fret son.

Don't ever again fret yourself.

Reprinted by kind permission of the Poet

From *'The Long Pale Corridor'*; edited by Judi Benson and Agneta Falk

Published by Boxdale Books

COPING WITH MY MOTHER'S DEATH

On September 26th, three years ago my mother was diagnosed with cancer. My whole family were devastated by the news, we couldn't believe it, and we thought there must be some mistake. Mum had never been sick in her life; she had regular check-ups and was very active. Now she had advanced stage cancer and only six months to live. This news, and the experience we were about to share as a family would change my life forever.

Mum loved people and was very involved in the community she was often called out when a death occurred in the town and would lay out the body, so we grew up with an awareness of death. She was passionate about Irish music and her all-time favourite pastime was bingo. Mum was my best friend and I went to her whenever I needed a shoulder to cry on or get advice. She was always there to pick up the pieces in good times and bad. Now I had to face the fact that Mum wasn't going to be around forever.

I felt immense sadness, panic, fear, anger and a tiny ray of hope that the doctors may be wrong (they weren't).

I wondered how I was going to cope. I thought about how cruel life was, how unfair that MY Mother had cancer. Then I realised I was only thinking about myself so I made a commitment to make Mum's last few months on earth as happy and comfortable as possible.

At about this time the Galway Hospice Home Care Team came into our lives and into our family. They were a huge help and gave us great support. They educated us on how to make Mum's journey towards death a happy one. For example; Mum was a very independent person and they explained that we couldn't suddenly take over all her decisions for her. My Mum had a great faith and was always a fighter; she wanted to get better and hadn't yet asked about her diagnosis.

That was her right and we would respect her wishes. Friends and family now became regular visitors at our home. Surprisingly, we had many happy days at this time, filled with music and laughter. Mum's best friend Nora, told stories about the pair of them as young women which we had never heard before. Bad days were still quite rare, and were usually around the distressing side effects of Mum's treatment such as chronic fatigue, constipation and hair loss.

One day Mum asked the doctor if she had cancer. When he told her "*yes*", there was a definite shift in her behaviour. A peaceful strength seemed to come over her and she was now ready to talk about what was happening. While this was a relief in one way it was also difficult and sad for the family. We were all aware that time was short and precious. There were things we wanted to say and do. The present mattered so much and Mum was getting noticeably weaker. Once Mum's deterioration began, it was very rapid. Her pain was well managed and she slept a lot, only staying awake for short periods at a time. On February 4th, she slipped into a gentle sleep and died. Nothing and nobody could soften the blow of her death. I had no Mother; she was gone from my life.

The days after her death were very busy as Mum's last wish was to be waked at home and then go to the church from her house. It was nice to know her wishes and to be able to carry them out.

When the funeral was over there was a period of desperate emptiness. Quietness had taken over a space that had being full of action, organisation and routines. I missed Mum dreadfully, her smile, her laughter, her friendship but was glad she had not been in great pain. I also felt fortunate to have been able to take leave from work and spend so much time with her. Friends became very important to me. I talked for hours on end, I cried, I needed to go over the story of Mum's illness again and again. The only comfort I had was knowing we had done all we could for her. There was no easy way out of my grief, no shortcuts, but good friends were a source of constant support to me. I believe that the time I spent with my mother during her illness helped me in my grief. She was a woman that gave so generously of herself and had so much to give that she left me with a positive sense of *"Live life for today and have no regrets"*. I like to think that her spirit lives on in me and that some day I will get involved in helping people who are bereaved.

Three years on I still have times of discouragement, exhaustion and sadness. I think this is normal. I survived those awful months of intense grieving and realised that the experience has changed me for the better. I feel I have more courage, I have lost my fear of death and I have beautiful memories of a wonderful woman whom I am privileged to say was my mother, Margaret. ▨

LOSS AND MEMORY

I stepped into her shoes. I became that person she always wanted me to be.

Standing in her kitchen , the sacred place of things that could not be touched, in front of me her private drawer of pieces of paper with "things "written on them, with her cooking utensils, measuring spoons and culinary implements . Drawers which always required her permission to open were now mine.

What were all these things for? Why where there so many different containers, vessels for cooking, dishes in a complex range of shapes and sizes? Why a person who chose everything so carefully and with a function in mind, should have all these objects so selected and collected and laid out in this manner.

It was not until a year after she died , almost to the day, when I opened Florence Greenberg and Evelyn Rose, the two great classical Jewish cookbooks to which she referred constantly, the more used and marked pages, a clue to those recipes which were most often consulted.

I started to cook in order to recreate all the foods that she had so lovingly and carefully created with such style for my father, in hope that feeding him with their particular taste, similarity, familiarity would make him eat and keep him alive.

Everything has a use, every plate comes to life as I cook for hours in my own clumsy way Every possible dish has its own pot. In spirit she stands inside me, my hands her hands. I peel, chop and stir my way into her memory.

Loss and Memory written by Amelia Stein

LOSS AND MEMORY, 2002

16 PHOTOGRAPHS

25 X 25CM

COLLECTION IRISH MUSEUM
OF MODERN ART

DONATION, IN MEMORY OF
MAENDEL STEIN, 2004

IN MEMORY OF MY MOTHER

I do not think of you lying in the wet clay
Of a Monaghan graveyard; I see
You walking down a lane among the poplars
On the way to the station, or happily

Going to second Mass on a summer Sunday-
You meet me and you say,
'Don't forget to see about the cattle';
Among your earthiest words the angels stray.

And I think of you walking along a headland
Of green oats in June,
So full of repose, so rich with life-
And I see us meeting at the end of a town

On a fair day by accident, after
The bargains are all made and we can walk
Together through the shops and stalls and markets
Free in the oriental streets of thought.

O you are not lying in the wet clay,
For it is a harvest evening now and we
Are piling up the ricks against the moonlight
And you smile up at us-eternally.

'In Memory of My Mother' is reprinted from *'Collected Poems'*, edited by Antoinette Quinn (Allen Lane 2004), by kind permission of the Trustees of the Estate of the late Katherine B. Kavanagh, through the Jonathan Williams Literary agency

ENDA, MY HERO

Enda was my hero. We faced a lot of challenges during the course of our marriage and throughout them all, Enda remained constant and strong. No other person has made such an impact on my life. Enda was, is, and will be, the person I most admire.

We met while playing tennis. I was playing in the Hodson Bay Hotel . . . my family's Hotel, and he drove up in a car with his friends. He always said that he remembered spotting me and saying to himself, 'I'd like to meet her'. And of course, we did meet and we fell in love and started a very passionate affair.

I was studying in UCD but I went home to Athlone on a regular basis and he came to Dublin to see me and we just couldn't get enough of each other. I would die for no one but him and he for no one but me. As soon as I finished my Degree I went straight back to Athlone to work in the family hotel and into Enda O'Rourke's arms.

We had quite a lot of rows, the kind of rows couples have when they are young and in love and we both picked up with other people from time to time before we settled down. We got married when I was 22 and he was 24 and in those days we were considered very young and people said that we had no sense and we probably didn't. I remember buying the engagement ring and I was just transfixed by it.

Naturally, I was very keen to have a baby and so was Enda but unlike my sister and brother who had produced a baby after only one year of marriage, we couldn't. Two and three years went by and still nothing and we were young and in love so it wasn't for lack of trying.

Eventually I got pregnant and gave birth to Feargal and it was during this period that I really thought Enda was wonderful because I went into a very deep post-natal depression. I felt terrible because this was the child we had longed for and I suddenly couldn't cope with the baby. My friends would ring me and invite me to meet them for coffee and I just thought 'I'll never get out of this house'.

Enda was so patient with me and so understanding and in the end I went up to Dublin and was prescribed medication and in a few months I was back to my old self.

Enda was very modern, he would always have been looking after Feargal although he didn't push the buggy, but I remember when I would measure out the baby formula he would always remind me to level out the spoon. I always felt we were equal in this enterprise, this marriage of Mary and Enda O'Rourke. A few years later my father suggested I do a, H Dip and become a teacher and Enda was the first to encourage me to go for it even though it involved traveling back and forth to Maynooth. He looked after Feargal while I went to college. He was very supportive.

A few months after we adopted our second son Aengus, Fianna Fail asked me to stand for my late father's seat but I said no, I wanted to be at home with my children. A few years later they asked again and this time Enda encouraged me to go for it. "Why wouldn't you?" he said. Years later when Charlie Haughey asked me to join the front bench he asked me, "Are you going to be serious about this?" I said that I was and he told me that I couldn't be driving up and down every day and advised me to arrange accommodation in Dublin and I thought that was very modern of him.

We would speak every day and I would tell him what was going on and he would tell me what was going on in Athlone. He always looked after the constituency for me, which was very important because in politics it is very difficult to trust people completely and of course I had total faith in him.

We had a very harmonious relationship, we were emotionally supportive of each other and of course our sexual relationship was always fantastic which I believe is very important in any marriage. Enda was never afraid to write down how he felt and would often send me love letters which I cherish.

Then it became my turn to look after him when he entered a period of ill-health and naturally I cared for him as best I could following his heart surgery.

Then after some years one Sunday evening, while watching the six o'clock evening news, he had a massive and fatal brain haemorrhage. He almost died in my arms. He was rushed to the Mater Hospital where he died in the early hours of January 30th 2001.

My grief is as intense now as it was then. I know I am not alone in feeling this way because I have spoken to other women who have lost their husbands. I think I have just built it into my life. I miss him desperately, I really do.

A year after I lost Enda, I lost my Dáil seat in Westmeath in the 2002 election. It was of course a devastating blow after decades of public life and serving for many years as a Minister with three portfolios. But it was just politics. The loss of votes is very different to the loss of a much loved husband.

I returned to politics by becoming a Senator and was appointed as Leader of Seanad Éireann in September 2002. There have been periods of political controversy in recent years where I have missed Enda's solid advice and support. I've often visited his grave and asked for some inspiration.

We used to spend every spare minute together and I miss his company on walks. At night, I miss his presence in the bed. I like to talk about him which can be disconcerting for people.

I know it is better to have lived and loved and there are very few real love stories in this world, mine is one of them.

Extract from an original article by journalist Helen Murray, published in The Sunday Tribune on 15th January 2006, and subsequently updated by Senator Mary O' Rourke

THE DEATH OF MY WIFE, MARIE

Marie and I had been married for 35 years when her health began to fail. Many visits to hospitals and to various consultants brought little improvement and I finally brought her to casualty on December 28th. Marie was admitted and stabilised over night. The next day, a Sunday, she was comfortable and smiling. She enjoyed a few family visitors and then, quietly and peacefully, she fell asleep and died. Neither of us had any idea that death was so near. But I know that the manner of her dying, quietly and without fuss, would have pleased her.

The funeral, amidst snow and ice, was a Godsend. It kept me busy for a month and I sailed along keeping up a façade of coping. I worried about how my daughters were coping. If the roles were reversed, Marie would have wept with them, consoled them and eased their pain. But I found that difficult to do.

At the end of January, my daughter returned to America and I was now in the house on my own. It was then that I really began to experience the pain of my grief. I felt lonely, sad and heartbroken. Many nights I cried myself to sleep, for the anguish of Marie's last few months were always with me.

I felt angry; angry with the doctors who appeared uncaring, and I felt guilty; guilty that I had not done enough for Marie. Above all I felt bewildered. Nothing in life had prepared me for this situation and I felt totally devastated.

Other people seemed to be able to cope with death. Why wasn't I? I began to think there was something wrong with me. Was I too soft or was I being irrational? I found it hard to remember the good times as people suggested I should do. All I could remember were days and weeks and months of poor health and crushing setbacks.

I missed Marie terribly. I wanted her to be there for our grandchildren and particularly for our daughter when she had a miscarriage. I felt so inadequate; Marie would have known how to support her.

After the funeral my own brothers and sister stopped mentioning Marie's name. It was as if she never existed. I know that they didn't want to add to my pain, but their reluctance to talk about her in those early days was puzzling and hurtful. I got a wonderful response when I plucked up the courage to talk to them about this. Now we can get together and reminisce about times we shared.

In many ways the second year of my bereavement was the most difficult, as I expected to be over the worst of it by then. I was only beginning to learn that the pain never goes away completely.

At one stage I yearned for companionship, but this has passed to some degree. I still feel wistful sometimes; especially when I see couples walking hand-in- hand or when I meet old friends of Marie's. These encounters can still leave me feeling sad.

I came to realise that I had done the best I could for Marie when she was ill, and I can now remember the happiness she brought into my life.

I remember her wonderful voice, her infectious laugh, and the many crazy times we went swimming in the sea at Donabate.

A number of years later, a long-closed window of my mind opened, when Marie's last conscious act surfaced in my memory for the first time. She could no longer speak, but as we left her hospital room that Sunday, she lifted her chin and tilting it higher with her fingers, she bade us with impish good humour to *"keep our chins up"*. Her farewell message; something to be remembered and cherished forever. So why had it remained hidden for so long? I can only conclude that the shock of her leaving, so suddenly and unexpectedly, had blanked it out, only for it to return when true and lasting healing had come about.

What helped me:

Finding someone who understood my pain and was prepared to listen no matter how long it took.

Setting small goals and challenges for myself to focus on (one was running in the city marathon at nearly 70 years of age)

Getting back into hobbies, such as walking and swimming, that I used to enjoy before Marie got sick.

What I learned from this experience:

I learned that the seemingly endless pain of bereavement does, in time, ease.

I learned that understanding can often be found in others who have had a similar bereavement

I found ways to strengthen and nourish a, once fragile, faith.

I learned to be less afraid of what may lie ahead for me.

Anne Madden

NIGHT PATHS

EXTRACT FROM THE ANNE MADDEN RETROSPECTIVE CATALOGUE RHA 1991

An Ethical Space

The Paintings of Anne Madden by Aidan Dunne

……It was in fact after yet another traumatic personal loss in 1984, that Madden was unable to work, and as she puts it herself, retreated "into a dark room", a dark room of the self. During this time she literally could not get herself into the studio. The path and garden paintings are hence literal descriptions of finding her way back to the studio. And of course it is tempting to see the dark-lit paths in the night paintings as leading to the "dark room", and the radiant passages of the daylight paintings as leading to the imaginative vitality of the studio. Doorways, openings, thresholds – as always they represent moments of decisive change, of initation, death, metamorphosis.……

NIGHT PATHS (TRIPTYCH), 1998

OIL ON CANVAS

195.7 X 292.1 CM

COLLECTION IRISH MUSEUM OF MODERN ART

DONATION, VINCENT AND NOELEEN FERGUSON, 1996

A YOUNG WIDOW'S STORY

As I stood in my living room staring out the window, the dark, dismal, rainy morning reflected every bit of what I was feeling inside. Outside the world continued on, people going to work, children going to school, the postman delivering letters. How could they? Why had everything not come to a stand still - my beloved, precious Paul was dead. My world had been ripped apart at the seams and my heart felt truly broken to pieces. I knew that life would never be the same again. There was a constant stream of visitors to the house, but in the midst of the crowd I felt so lonely and alone. I felt sad, numb and angry. I was angry with everyone, including Paul, who had left me here to pick up the pieces of our shattered dreams. This wasn't how it was meant to be, this wasn't the future we had planned.

Even the smallest tasks like having a shower and making breakfast seemed overwhelming. Every day was a struggle. In the early days, I was very caught up in the children's needs and felt I had to shelve my own grief. Everybody seemed to be avoiding mentioning Paul's name and yet my children desperately needed to talk about their Daddy. Maybe 'the adults' felt it would be too painful or upsetting for them to hear his name- could they not have asked the children what they wanted?

My greatest fear early on was that my brain would wipe away the memories of Paul. I panicked if I couldn't recall his face for a moment. I was also plagued with guilt as I remembered whispering to Paul at the end that it was OK for him to let go of life and that I would be all right. Did he feel I had given up on him? It took a long time for me to accept that I had done the best thing for Paul; that he needed to feel free to stop struggling.

I was so used to taking care of Paul during his illness that I now felt useless and abandoned. I also found it difficult to cope with remarks from people that I was "young and strong" and that I would "get over it". I didn't want to "get over it". I wasn't interested in a future without Paul.

In the early months after Paul's death, I felt my grief ravaging through every second of my days and nights. It seeped into every bone of my body. It was as if a tidal wave of emotion had poured through me, there was no escaping it. I wanted the world to stop so I could get off for a while.

Many months after Paul's death, I reached a turning point. I made a conscious decision to make Paul an on-going part of my life and the children's life; but in a new way. We now looked at photos and talked about happy and sad times we'd had together. My children loved hearing stories about their Daddy when he was young. I was slowly beginning to wake up with feelings of hope that I might have a future. I began to balance despair with hope, tears with laughter and bad times with good times.

When Paul's first anniversary came around, I was shocked at the intensity of the feelings that emerged again. After all, this was a year down the road and people seemed to expect me to be back to normal. I realised then that I would always grieve for Paul, that the pain of this loss would never truly leave me. But I have come to accept the changes that his death has brought to my life. I am open to new experiences and I know now that I have a future.

What helped me:

Writing about Paul's death; I used my writing to express my loneliness, my desperation and my panic. I also tried to get down on paper as many precious memories as I could.

People in my life who simply listened, with patience and respect to whatever I had to say. People who didn't try to "make me feel better".

Availing of Bereavement Support in the Hospice where Paul died.

Allowing myself to have a "bad day" even long after the 1st anniversary of Paul's death had passed.

Going for long walks on the beach or in the park and listening to music.

What I learned through Paul's illness and death:

I learned that when you love someone they never fully leave you.

I learned that death is not separate from life and I am frightened by it no longer.

I learned that grief is like a journey - I had to be patient, understanding and kind to myself along the way.

I learned that it was important to talk openly with my children even though they were very young. I tried to answer their questions honestly, and I found they were OK with me crying and being sad sometimes.

I learned that I needed to grieve in my own way, and that nobody else could fully understand what it was like for me.

Adrienne Lord

"THE PRESENCE OF ABSENCE/PASSAGE OF TIME"

These images are from an exhibition entitled "The Presence of Absence/Passage of Time". It was the culmination of work I did in the years following the death of my husband on the 3rd of August 1998. We were on holiday in Kerry with his family when he had a heart attack and died on the beach. It was a terrible shock. Nothing had prepared us for this. We muddled on, incubated ourselves for a bit, but life continued around us. My daughter got her leaving results and started college. My son went back to school and I went back to Art College.

It was like a bad dream. I buried myself in sorting things out and looking after my children. At the same time I was under pressure to produce work in college. Finding it hard to come to terms with what had happened, I started work based on his wardrobe of clothes. It seemed the only tangible thing left of him.

Five years after he died I decided to have an exhibition of this work because at the time I found it very difficult to find information about support. So with the help of a bereavement therapist we used the show as an opportunity to provide talks on different types of loss and invited various groups and organisations working in the area of bereavement to take part and to provide information on their services. It was hard, but in doing this I managed to make something positive out a very difficult experience and it helped me come to terms with my own loss.

"THE PRESENCE OF ABSENCE/PASSAGE OF TIME"

ADRIENNE LORD

REPRINTED BY KIND PERMISSION OF THE ARTIST

TURNING GRIEF AROUND

Ten years ago my husband died. He died suddenly, without warning, following a complicated, but routine operation. That day a world opened which I had never imagined before.

From the moment the hospital rang asking me to come in urgently; I knew my husband was dead. I did not know what to do. Nothing like this had ever happened to me before. Nothing like this had happened to my friends. In the world of the day before, these things happened only in films.

I remember looking over at my two young sons as I put the phone down, thinking: *"I don't have to tell them this. I can just pretend nothing has happened."* Because once I told them, their childhood would be over and we would be plunged into a world that would never be the same again. It was then that I made a resolution: however bad this would be, we were going to meet it head-on. Whatever the degree of pain, we would do what was necessary to get through it. That meant, first of all, not being afraid. It was as if I understood, instinctively, that the worst enemy would not be pain, but fear.

Still, when the shock wore off, the pain was intense; so bad at times I could not even find a physical position that was comfortable – much less eat or sleep. But I learned to say to myself; *"it is only pain. It is not good or bad, but a sign we have been wounded. If we pay attention to the wound, if we do not ignore it, we will heal"*. Within the year, people started asking me questions such as; *"Have you recovered yet?"* *Recovered what?* I would ask myself. My world had disappeared with my husband. Like many widows, I had not only lost a husband and a father to our children, but also income and status. Invitations had started to dry up. The phone calls fell off. My husband's friends, with notable exceptions, avoided me. Out of the corner of my eye, I would glimpse people crossing the street so they did not have to meet me. *"Have you begun dating again?"* What?! How do you begin dating when you haven't dated for over thirty years? When you are trying to hold down a full-time professional job, raise two now vulnerable boys, and hold on to your sanity?

My mind was no longer my own. It was entirely preoccupied by questions: such as *"What do I do now? Where is all this going?"* As I am clearly not going to *recover* – in the sense that things are never going to be the same again – what direction is open to me? Why are there no maps? Why, when everyone at some time or another is going to go through this experience – and not only once – has someone not plotted out some routes for the journey?

Instead of routes, what society offered me were deflections: a whole catechism of clichés as threadbare as they were useless. *"Time will heal", "You'll get over it".* Clearly, the world's plan was for me to enter into cliché myself. It was a conspiracy: I would act the poor, mousey, perhaps pious widow and allow them to inflict these aphorisms on me in the interests of my wellbeing. I might even agree: *"Oh yes, how kind of you. Of course time will heal. I am almost recovered now. Anyway, as you say, it's the will of God – so I should just get on with the suffering he has inflicted on me and my family."* Then someone told me there *was* a map; it was called The Stages of Grief. It told me I would go through different emotional reactions in a predictable order, beginning with Denial and ending with Acceptance. Very tidy. Now I could get on with it – suffering by schedule. Except when I tried to pay attention to them, the Stages got all mixed up – if I could identify them at all. As far as I could see, Denial would veer suddenly into Acceptance and then back again into Anger. I dared not believe in Hope. Bargaining did not come into it at all. With whom or for what could I bargain? My husband was dead – nothing could bring him back. In the end, what reading about the Stages of Grief did was make me feel even more a failure. First I had lost my husband. Now, according to this plan, I couldn't even grieve for him properly.

Meanwhile, I was still lost – and incredulous that such a powerful, absorbing experience should be so little valued that no one had thought to mark routes through its treacherous reefs and shoals.

Then one day I attended a talk on helping children through bereavement by Barbara Monroe, the Director of St Christopher's Hospice in London. On the table before her was a very large glass jar. Beside it were three balls: one large, one medium-sized, one small. Without a word, she began to stuff the large ball into the jar. With a great deal of effort, she wedged it in. Then she held the jar up. *"There!"* she said. *"That's how grieving feels at first. If grief is the ball and the jar is your world, you can see how the grief fills everything. There is no air to breathe, no space to move around. Every thought, every action reminds you of your loss."*

Then, with great effort, she pulled the large ball out of the jar and put in the medium-sized ball. She held it up again, tipping it so the ball rolled around a bit. *"Maybe you think that's how it will feel after a time – say, after the first year. Grieving will no longer fill every bit of space in your life."* Then she rolled the ball out and plopped in the small ball, holding up the jar again.

"Now, say, by the second or third year, that's how grieving is supposed to feel. Like the ball, it has shrunk. So now you can think of grief as taking up a very small part of your world – it could almost be ignored if you wish to ignore it."

I settled back into my seat. Two more glass jars were produced from under the table: one larger, one larger still. Silently, she took the largest ball and squeezed it slowly into the smallest of the three jars. It would barely fit.

Then she pulled the ball out and placed it in the next-largest jar. There was room for it to roll around. Finally, she took it out and dropped it into the largest glass jar. *"There,"* she said, *"That's what grieving is really like. If your grieving is the ball, like the ball here it doesn't get any bigger or any smaller. It is always the same. But the jar is bigger. If your world is this glass jar, your task is to make your world bigger."*

"You see," she continued, *"no one wants their grief to shrink. It is all they have left of the person who died. But if your world gets larger, then you can keep your grief as it is, but work around it."*

Then she turned to us. *"I work with children. Children are lucky, because their world is always getting bigger. But older people coping with grief often try to keep their world the same. It is a mistake. If I have one thing to say to all of you it is this: Make your world larger. Then there will be room in it for your grieving, but your grieving will not take up all the room. This way you can find space to make a new life for yourselves."*

how others see grieving   how you can grow through grief

That was eight years ago And I notice now how large my world has become since then. The 'balls-and-jars' gave me a new way of imagining grieving – and how it might be turned around. It seemed to me that surely there must be other metaphors that could help.

When I first came to Ireland as a young wife, I had to learn to cope with a new country, now my husband's death had transported me to what felt like yet another foreign land. I was lost; I didn't know my way around; I didn't know the rules. People took to asking me whether I was selling the house and *"going home." "This is my home"*, I would insist. If grieving is like enforced emigration, there is a history, both mine and that of others, that tells us it is not only about loss. Anyone who has lived in America for any time knows the stories of those who have immigrated there. And, for all their pain, they tell how, in the end, the new country gave a chance for new lives, ones in which the old lives were not entirely abandoned.

This metaphor enabled me not only to survive, but gradually, like so many displaced people, to thrive. Having emigrated long before in my head to a place where I am neither married nor unmarried, neither desolate nor jubilant, I am now literally in a new country, China – and here enlarging my life.

Graphics; Sarah John; by kind permission of Darton Longman and Todd

■ *"GRIEVING: A BEGINNER'S GUIDE"* BY JERUSHA HULL McCORMACK IS RECENTLY PUBLISHED BY PARACLETE. A SHORT HANDBOOK TO HELP PEOPLE THROUGH THE GRIEVING PROCESS, IT COMBINES MEDITATIONS ON THE NATURE OF GRIEF ALONG WITH PRACTICAL ADVICE ON HOW BEST TO MAKE ONE'S WAY THROUGH THIS JOURNEY INTO A NEW LIFE.

Eiléan Ní Chuilleanáin

A HAND, A WOOD

MY SISTER MÁIRE WHO DIED IN 1990 WAS A PROFESSIONAL
VIOLINIST IN THE LONDON PHILHARMONIC ORCHESTRA.
HER ASHES ARE IN A WOOD IN ITALY.

1

After three days I have to wash –
I am prising you from under my nails
Reluctantly, as time will deface
The tracks, their branching sequence,
The skill of the left and the right hand.

Your script curls on the labels of jars,
Naming pulses in the kitchen press.
The dates you marked in the diary come and pass.

2

The wet leaves are blowing, the sparse
Ashes are lodged under the trees in the wood
Where we cannot go in this weather,
The stream is full and rattling,
The hunters are scattering shot—
The birds fly up and spread out.

I am wearing your shape
Like a light shirt of flame;
My hair is full of shadows.

Reprinted by kind permission of the author and The Gallery Press
From *'The Brazen Serpent'*

THE DEATH OF MY SISTER, PAULINE

Growing up in Limerick, my sister, Pauline and I were always very close, but it was not until we both got married and had daughters of our own that we became best friends. Pauline had a brain haemorrhage at the age of thirty-nine and never regained her full health. One thing that stood out about Pauline was that she had a beautiful voice and loved to sing. Her favourite songs were: *"One day at a time"* and *"So deep is the night"*, and we would sing these in the car on our many journeys to and from the hospital. Following the death of our mother, Pauline became very depressed and seemed to lose her will to live. I was living in Dublin rearing my own family at the time, and couldn't always see her as often as I wished. On the 15th of January Pauline had a massive heart attack. I will never forget that day. I got a phone call to say she had been taken ill. Half an hour later, I got a second call to say the hospital had been unable to resuscitate her and she was dead. I was distraught as I set out for the long drive to Limerick. The weather matched the way I felt, torrential rain that never let up. It broke my heart going into the family home that night, knowing that Pauline would never again be sitting in her favourite chair, smoking a cigarette. I thought about how her face used to light up when she saw me coming and I couldn't believe that I would never see her again. I thought about how much I would miss the "day-to-dayness" of our relationship. I remembered how we would catch up on the week's events, gossiping, and doing all the things that best friends do together. What made all this more difficult was that I never got the chance to say goodbye. I felt cheated.

Pauline's husband was inconsolable and I had no words of comfort for him because my own heart was breaking. I ended up having to make a lot of the funeral arrangements. Until you are in the situation you don't realise how much there is to do; people to contact, decisions to make. The next few days were some of the hardest in my life. Seeing my sister, my best friend laid out in her coffin was devastating. The day before her funeral, Pauline's son-in-law asked me to go with him to the garage, as he wanted to show me something. He took out a green plastic bag and asked me what he should do with it. When I looked inside all I saw were rags. When I looked again, I realised they were Pauline's clothes. I knew the hospital had had to cut through her clothes when they were trying to save her life. But the sight of her beautiful clothes cut to ribbons was truly upsetting and brought to mind vivid images that I didn't want. Another very difficult time was Pauline's birthday. Because she died so close to her birthday, the family already had a surprise party planned for her. But now instead of the party, we held a commemorative Mass.

Pauline's death hit me harder than the deaths of either of my parents and I missed her sorely as time went on. I spent a lot of time in Limerick with her family and while I was there I never let my feelings show. I felt, mistakenly, that I had to be strong for others. It was only when I came back up to Dublin that I would let myself cry and be sad. I forced myself to sing the old songs she loved and when I was able to do this without breaking down I knew I was beginning to cope with my grief and starting to accept her absence in my life.

Pauline came to me in a dream one night and told me to be happy for her, that she was in a better place and that she was at peace. Some people may find that a bit strange but it was an experience that helped me come to terms with her death. I am quite a spiritual person and I sometimes feel her presence around me, which is comforting. I still talk to her and ask for her help and guidance when life gets tough

I miss Pauline. Although I have made good friends as an adult, Pauline knew me all my life, we had shared a childhood together, she remembered me as a little girl and that was special. I still feel sad when I visit certain places or hear a certain song that reminds me of her. One positive thing that came out of Pauline's death was a much closer relationship with my other sister. Our grief brought us together in a way that wouldn't have happened otherwise. I have come to accept that Pauline is gone and I will never see her again on earth. There is still, and always will be, a void in my life, a place no one else can fill. But I am thankful for having had her in my life, and I know that because of her, I am a gentler, less-judgemental person. ▨

Seamus Heaney

THE LIFT

A first green braird; the hawthorn half in leaf.
Her funeral filled the road
And could have stepped from some old photograph.

Of a Breton *pardon*, remote
Familiar women and men in caps
Walking four abreast, soon falling quict.

The came the throttle and articulate whops
Of a helicopter crossing, and afterwards
Awareness of the sound of our own footsteps,

Of open air, and the life behind those words
'Open' and 'air'. I remembered her aghast,
Foetal, shaking, sweating, shrunk, wet-haired,

A beaten breath, a misting mask, the flash
Of one wild glance, like a ghost surveillance
From behind a gleam of helicopter glass.

A lifetime, then the deathtime: reticence
Keeping us together when together,
All declaration deemed outspokenness.

Favourite aunt, good sister, faithful daughter,
Delicate since childhood, tough alloy
Of disapproval, kindness and *hauteur,*

She took the risk, at last, of certain joys –
Her birdtable and jubilating birds,
The 'fashion' in her wardrobe and her tallboy.

Weather, in the end, would say our say.
Reprise of griefs in summer's clearest mornings,
Children's deaths in snowdrops and the may,

Whole requiems at the sight of plants and gardens…
They bore her lightly on the bier. Four women,
Four friends – she would have called them girls –
   stepped in

And claimed the final lift beneath the hawthorn.

Reprinted by kind permission of the Poet
From *'District and Circle'* published by Faber and Faber Ltd

LOSS IN THE TRAVELLER COMMUNITY

'I lost my eldest son 25 year ago, he was killed in England and he was called Kieran, Kieran Collins, he was 13 at the time. My brother's son was killed at the same time. He was 15; Michael. It was a month before my eighth child was born. I'll never forget the day; it was the 20th of June; it was on a Sunday. He went out the door that morning along with a whole lot of his friends and Michael his cousin with him. About 3 o clock that day (it was a lovely warm day) I seen the policeman approaching our house. Me and me husband we asked him what's wrong and he said; "have ye got a son called Kieran", I says "yeah". He says; "will you come inside," we were out the front of the house, he told us he says; "he's dead".

I didn't know what happened, I remember me husband roarin, but I passed out and ended up in the neighbour's house next door, I remember comin around after someone giving me brandy on a spoon. My husband was goin over to my brother's house who lived a few streets away and they were roarin about their son after bein killed. Their youngest, my eldest. We brought them home to Ireland to bury them, the two were buried together. I suppose at that time, and I suppose up to this present day, I never really got over it and I never will because, put it this way, it hits me everyday of the week especially at Christmas and birthdays. I still have to go and visit his grave regular; I even came home from England. I have to chat with him. I love to look after the grave.

How did I cope? I was a stronger woman at the time and had other childer, I knew I had to keep goin for them. Me faith helped me a lot. I went to healing places and shrines and prayed to God to give me strength in order to look after my family. I could not look at his picture, I loved to, but couldn't for at least 14 year. Then I eventually started looking at his picture. Doctors wanted to give me sleeping tablets for my nerves but my mother said 'don't start takin them Missie because you'll have to start comin to terms'. I don't think I ever came to terms, but just that my own family and extended family kept me goin. My husband never came to terms with it, he couldn't visit the grave and walked away from it cryin. I lost him five year ago, we were very close and the rest of me family were very close to their Daddy. We are not the same since that happened either, the support is gone, the boys were very attached to him, and the girls as well. I think all that keeps us goin is the graves, both of them are buried together. We go and fix the graves. We're a very lonely family.

Just to say; anyone that loses a family member is never the same again. There's a part of that family missing. Time heals a bit but you never forget.' ▨

This story was dictated by Missie Collins to staff at Pavee Point

Carol Ann Duffy

FUNERAL

Say milky cocoa we'd say,
you had the accent for it,
drunk you sometimes would. *Milky*

cocoa Preston. We'd all
laugh. *Milky cocoa*. Drunk,
drunk. You laughed, saying it.

From all over the city
mourners swarmed, a demo against
death, into the cemetery.

You asked for nothing.
Three gravediggers, two minutes
of silence in the wind. Black

cars took us back. Serious
drinking. Awkward ghosts
getting the ale in. All afternoon

we said your name, repeated
the prayers of anecdotes,
bereaved and drunk

enough to think you might arrive,
say *milky cocoa... Milky*
cocoa, until we knew you'd gone.

Reprinted by kind permission of the Poet
From *'The Long Pale Corridor'*; edited by Judi Benson and Agneta Falk
Published by Boxdale Books

DOROTHY

Dorothy, 2003, was painted by Sean Scully in memory of his friend, the art critic, Dorothy Walker.

DOROTHY, 2003

OIL ON LINEN

274.5 X 335CM

COLLECTION IRISH MUSEUM OF MODERN ART

HERITAGE GIFT BY LOCHLANN AND BRENDA QUINN, 2005

COURTESY KERLIN GALLERY, DUBLIN

AIDAN'S DEATH

I was there when Aidan was born and I was the first to be told that he had been killed 25 years later.

I vividly remember the Angelus bell tolling at 6 o clock on January 19th 1966, on our grainy black and white rented television; and a couple of seconds later hearing a new baby's cry from the upstairs bedroom.

Aidan was born at home, 8 days before my tenth birthday.

This meant that, with a large family, I was at the right age to "mind" him.

So I was assigned the sometimes onerous task of wheeling Aidan around Claddagh Green for the first few years of his life.

Even after he began walking, he was entrusted to my care.

And yes, as I was hitting my teenage years, most of my peers carried a hurley, a hoola hoop or a football – I always arrived attached to Aidan.

Yes we were close.

On the Sunday before he died he had bemoaned to me the dilapidated state of his company van – kicking the front wheel in anger.

Four days later that same front wheel collapsed, Aidan lost control, his van careered under a truck on the Maynooth road and in the ensuing mayhem; Aidan died – as did a young Spanish woman travelling behind.

I was just about to go into a radio studio and remarked that the crash in Maynooth sounded awful.

When I arrived up from studio at 2.45, I was met by the RTE Chaplin and a friend who told me Aidan had been killed.

I remember remarking it would kill my mother – her youngest child was dead.

I phoned our next door neighbour in Claddagh green who told me my mother was sitting in the back garden on a kitchen chair, enjoying the afternoon sun.

Driving to Ballyfermot I tried to recite a formula of words to tell my mother Aidan had been killed.

She knew when she opened the front door – that something was drastically wrong.

And then the screams, the pleadings, the supplications to God Almighty for it not be true.

My other brothers arrived, deeply, deeply traumatised.

One brother had only waved to Aidan in traffic a couple of hours before the tragedy.

My 87 year old grandmother arrived, intoning as to why God had not taken her instead.

Friends arrived – and yes, their presence does make a difference.

We did get a grip on the funeral – really important.

We insisted on carrying Aidan's coffin from the family home to the local church – his friends taking turns in a public display of physical support.

We did participate strongly in the liturgy – and spoke about Aidan from the altar – and yes, it did make a difference.

But the wound won't heal.

That he was exactly ten years younger than me meant that my every single birthday lies in the shadow of Aidan's.

When I was forty he would have been celebrating his thirtieth birthday.

My mother still winces at the news of every single car crash.

She still reveres his grave – as we all do.

We still weep at all that might have been for dear Aidan.

Other people are heaven when it comes to bereavement, just being there; even fumbled, awkward words are a solace.

Whatever you say – or don't say to the bereaved, it will make a difference.

Sympathy cards, notes and letters did also make an impact – in time.

Being there – in whatever way you can – is what matters.

Yes, I am afraid of death, but I am no longer afraid of consoling or grieving. ⌘

Joe Duffy, Nov 2006

WHAT IS IT ALL ABOUT?

What were you thinking my love when you drew this? I can imagine you in your studio, standing at the drawing board, working deftly with the crayons. Big bold strokes of yellow and black. An enormous ball, perhaps a meteor out of the blue, hits a solitary, ordinary house and knocks it off its blocks.

Tumbling is one of a number of drawings and sculptures my wife Aileen MacKeogh did in the late 1980s. They formed part of her exhibition *House*. Many of the drawings were based on images of houses under attack.

She started this series of work two years after our son Luke died. One ordinary day he twisted out of the arms of our babysitter and fell down the stairs in our house. He died two days later. He was 10 months old. Our lives were blown apart. All the security and comfort of our house and home came tumbling down.

In all her work, Aileen tried to capture the things that lie beneath the surface. In the *House* work she was trying to bring to the surface the feelings of fragility and insecurity that lie beneath the surface of our lives. Our houses may seem strong and solid, but houses become homes and homes are very vulnerable. Homes are built on feelings and emotions. In the sculptures that accompanied the drawings Aileen captured the way in which we transform bare rooms and walls into places full of beauty and meaning. We pour ourselves into our homes. They become sanctuaries, places of comfort and consolation from which we can escape the slings and arrows of our lives. Our houses are our retreats from the world, our heavens in a heartless world. Within the interior of our homes we explore the interiors of our lives. We take off the masks we wear outside. We love and care. We pour out our hearts..

But the *House* work was really all about Luke. It was about the enormous pain and sense of loss that welled up in Aileen after he died. A woman who knew little of nothing about grief was suddenly overwhelmed by it. It took two years before the rawness of the pain began to ease and she was able to start working again.

She was able to harness the experience of grief and, using her artistic creativity, find a way not just of expressing that pain but of saying something deeply significant about our lives, the spaces in which we live, and the way in which we create meaning and beauty. It would be wrong to think that Aileen's grief was a means to being artful; or that her art was a means of grieving. They came together to express her ideas about life.

Aileen died of breast cancer eighteen months ago. I have no idea why. I have no idea what this life is all about. But I do know that we are compelled to love and care for each other as much as we can. I do know that those of us who deeply experience grief feel that compulsion all the more.

I cannot draw. I seek comfort, consolation and hope in words. Since Aileen died I have learned to talk and write about my feelings for her, for what has happened to me, to Luke, and the life we had. Of course I feel a huge sense of loss, but I recognise more than ever the need for love. It is painful. I still sleep in the same bed where Aileen died. I walk up and down the stairs where Luke fell. I feel that they were both so unlucky. Although there are many sad memories in this house, it also resounds with beauty and happiness. I still have so much. Shortly before she died Aileen told me she wanted me to be happy and to be in love. I live in hope. 🖼

Aileen MacKeogh

TUMBLING

Tumbling, from the exhibition *House*

Reprinted by kind permission of The estate of the late Aileen MacKeogh

WHEN ROBERTA DIED

Roberta Gray took her own life on New Year's Day 2006, aged 28. Best known to the public as an accomplished journalist, both documenting life as a young person in Dublin and writing on and reviewing the arts, she also appeared on radio and television. More recently she had turned her attention to the environment, one of the first Irish journalists to do so.

A loving daughter and sister, she had a wide circle of friends formed through her many interests. Always adventurous and quite fearless, she loved to travel and experience the differences of life lived elsewhere. The depression which she had fought so bravely during her adult years finally claimed her at a time when she was working to restructure her working life in order to give more time to issues of wellbeing and environmental projects. At the time of her death she had almost completed her training to qualify as a teacher of Iyengar yoga.
A colourful, caring individual she was in all things true to herself. Her death, which came as a terrible shock to us all, has left an enormous gap in the lives of everyone who knew and loved her.

This is the story of how we, Roberta's parents, have tried to manage in the months since our daughter died. It's an account of some practical strategies which we worked out as time went by. Our emotional healing, slower to begin and different for each of us, may take a lot longer to complete.

From the very first hours following Roberta's suicide, as we realised that something appalling had happened, we also knew that we were already taking the first steps along a road which was completely foreign and uncharted for us. But in those same hours, a circle of comforting support was already beginning to form around the family. Once the news of her death became widespread, we were overwhelmed by acts of kindness and offers of help – many of which we gladly accepted. All this was new for us, we didn't know what to expect, but we followed our instincts and vowed to look after ourselves, to keep strong for the journey ahead. Both retired, we were lucky to have the loving care and support of each other, although there were times, particularly at the beginning, when the structure and company of work might have been a help too.

Friends often said that they couldn't imagine how we felt, while others just asked how we were feeling. In truth, we didn't really know. The routine of coping with each day left us little time to brood, and it was only when we went away a month later to be with our son in San Francisco that the lonely reality of what had happened began to make itself felt. Yet being there in sunshine and that wonderful scenery was good for the soul, especially then, in February, when all could have been so grey back home in Ireland.

On our return we started to face into the many tasks which awaited, while beginning to pick up the threads of our own lives again. Bridge, choir and walking all helped us to reintegrate and provided an escape from the overwhelming sense of grief and loss which surrounded us at home. I began to feel as if I'd been hit by a bus as my body emerged from its state of shock, so I took up the yoga that I'd let slip three months previously and soon began to feel more relaxed and able to cope. Music too gave us the solace which we so badly needed and even if it sometimes meant the effort of going out to a public performance, we knew that once there we could be privately reflective. The garden, coming to life again after the winter, gave us glimmerings of hope for the year to come and we began to spend more time there making preparations for the summer's crops.

We spent several weeks replying to the hundreds of messages which we'd received after Roberta's death, finding this immensely therapeutic, if exhausting, as we could now personally address many of her friends and colleagues whom we knew hardly, if at all. We got together with our own friends; spending quiet evenings together and soon began to see some of Roberta's closest friends occasionally. Remembering that our grief was their's also, it was good to spend time sharing memories with them. They were a wonderful, and vital, support to us in giving us a broader picture of our daughter in her adult life.

As we tired easily, we limited how much we did each day, yet tried to ensure that we had something planned for each weekend, the loneliest of times. We discovered that there is a very fine line between being sufficiently occupied to avoid time for brooding, and over-activity which could lead to tearful exhaustion. Each day is different, so we still steer a middle course and hope to stay upright. We find that it helps to have some sort of schedule so that we can arrange to meet up with people at a time that fits in, rather than feeling pressurised into doing more than we feel able. Fatigue has been a major effect of our bereavement and, nine months on, we are still not completely back to full strength.

So how do we feel now? Our grief is always with us, but we bear it in different ways. Gradually our ability to get on with life seems stronger now, though we are still very vulnerable to unexpected moments of sorrow. As Roberta's work was so public we often find ourselves unbearably reminded of her absence as we look at the papers, flick on the television, or note the announcement of some organic/environmental festival or rock concert. We know she should be there. But her spirit is always with us, in both glad times and sad. We laugh and remember good moments together – like the day we saw a pink fridge in a shop in Dublin, smiled at each other and said simultaneously "Roberta would have *loved* that!"

Caroline Gray, Dundrum, 28 September 2006

■ ROBERTA'S PARENTS, CAROLINE AND PATRICK GRAY, RETIRED LIBRARIAN AND SECONDARY TEACHER RESPECTIVELY, LIVE IN DUBLIN. THEIR SON, NICHOLAS, CURRENTLY WORKS IN SAN FRANCISCO.

BLACK DOG IN MY DOCS DAY

IN MEMORY OF MY NEPHEW MICHAEL MULLINS (SLIM-2-SPEED)
WHO DIED ON 9TH DECEMBER 1999 AGED 18 YEARS AND
11 MONTHS

Your mother rings from your grave.
I say where are you?
She says, I'm at Michael's grave
and it looks lovely today.

Duffy misses you,
Jennifer Lydon misses you.
You were grand until depression
slipped into your shoes —
after that you dragged your feet
big long giraffe strides. Slim-2 Speed.

When depression slept
you were up for anything,
go for it and you went for it —
times you got it, other times you lost it,
you didn't play the lyre,
you played the horses,
lady luck was often with you
you never looked back
William and Lara miss you.

When you were a few months old
I went to see you in hospital,
you had meningitis.
The nurse told me that I had to leave,
I told her you were my nephew,
she said you still had meningitis.
You had days months and years to go,
the crowd in Maxwell's miss you.

When your mother said,
Michael started school today
I thought you were too young,
you grew up without telling us,
you went to sleep small,
when you got up
you were kitchen-table tall,
you had fourteen years to go.

A messer in your Communion photos,
leaning against the wall in hidden valley
arms akimbo, one foot behind the other,
you were ready to trip the light fantastic
the body of Christ.

Odd times in Castle Park
when you were passing the house,
I'd said, Michael wait up
you'd say, no way José!
I've got the black dog in my shoes
I have to drag him half way across Ireland,
I have to do it today and it must be raining.

Our Jennifer misses you
Christy misses the long chats with you,
he wished you didn't talk so much in the bookies,
Heather misses you,
Larry didn't know you
but Larry misses you because Heather misses you.
Eleven years to go you dyed your hair,
your uncles didn't know you,
they didn't know what they were missing.
No school wanted you.
You wanted Nirvana, you wanted The Doors,
you wanted shoes you didn't have to drag
you wanted hush puppies or Gandhi's flip-flops
instead you got Docs with a difference
the joy-roy gang miss you.

For your Confirmation
you took Hercules as your middle name,
you wanted a sweatshirt and baggy pants,
you left your mother and George at the church,
kiss me there you said to your mother
pointing to your cheek
and you were off with your fiends,
soldier of Christ.
Auntie Mary and Aidan miss you,
Johnny misses you,
Caroline Keady misses you.

Móinín na gCiseach Tech said you failed maths,
you went in yourself to set the record straight.
Your mother has the letter of apology the school sent.
No school wanted the boy with blue hair
Dana C. and Caroline L. miss you.

You did the junior cert
with 'Dóchas an Oige',
we went down on open day,
you made us cranky buns,
real conversation stoppers.
Bobby and Shane miss you.

The day you and I filled in
your passport application
your shoes were empty
except for your long dreamy feet,
they matched your fanciful answers.
Name: Michael drop-dead-gorgeous Mullins.
Who do you want to be when you grow up?
A rolling fucking stone baby
Keith The Buckfast Kid misses you,
Margaret and John miss you.

The black dog came and went,
he didn't answer to Lassie
but when you said, hey Cerberus!
an idiotic grin came over his dogface.
The tea-leaf who just got out misses you.

When I visited you in the Psych first
you were outside sitting next to
a bucketful of cigarette ends.
I said you'd need to cut down
on the fags or you'd end up killing yourself.
We laughed till we nearly cried.
Granny Bernie misses you
Alice and Brendan miss you
you had a year left give or take.

You talked a lot about your daughter Erin,
she was eighteen months you were eighteen years.
You were here she was over there.
You called to Father Frankie
and asked if one day you could have Erin baptised,
you were soaking to the skin that day,
you were always walking in the rain,
docs filled with despair day,
black dog in my docs day.
Jackie from the psych misses you.

The day you got out for the last time
you and I walked from our house to Carnmore.
We had a drink at the crossroads
You weren't supposed to with the medication.
Fuck it you said if all those smarties I took
didn't kill me a pint of pissie beer hardly will.

You showed me round the house,
you said it was spooky,
and if you were going to top yourself
it would be here you'd do it, and you did.
Auntie Carmel in Florida misses you,
Jennifer said you had a girlfriend,
Linda misses you,
Claire from Waterside House misses you.

You wanted to fathom the world
but your legs were tired,
you had two months left.
Cookie and Jillian miss you.
You talked about the dark hole
you often found yourself in,
you were happy when you got out
but when you were in it,
there was no talking to you,
you had weeks to go.
The Rinnmore gang miss you.

You got a bad 'flu
and the 'flu got you
the Millennium Bug,
your days were numbered.

Depression and the 'flu didn't travel
but you did and you never came back.
On December the 9th 1999
you hanged yourself.
Paddy L. and Michael Flaherty miss you.

Your mother rings from your grave
I say where are you?
She says, I'm at Michael's grave
and it looks lovely today.

Reprinted by kind permission of the poet
From 'An Awful Racket'
Published by Bloxdale Books

CORMAC'S DEATH

It is so strange, writing those words starkly for the first time; I have so often spoken of his death, but usually I've been asked questions, or prompted. it's one of those moments when it hits me; the cold, unbelievable reality of it all.

The night Cormac died, the shock and numbness I experienced were indescribable, and yet I had to act while there was still hope – to try to waken my sleeping son, having just breathed his last, but with half-open eyes staring into space. *"I think the poor child's dead"*, the awful words of my husband Brendan, which I never imagined I'd hear. *"God has taken him"*, was my first thought, but we continued to take action; ringing the ambulance, trying resuscitation, and ringing a neighbouring doctor and the priest. As all this happened I tried to shut down my panic and despair, and for the ninety minutes that followed, we tried to pray, and, just suppressed the combination of blind panic and emptiness that filled us. I also remember saying to myself, that if it was his time to go, I shouldn't be trying to keep him here on earth. With the end of those ninety minutes, and of hope, I was wrapped in a cocoon of numbness and resignation; one I have never completely come out of.

Brendan, in those first couple of hours, with presence of mind and courage, telephoned neighbours, family, the Tyrone Gaelic football manager, Mickey Harte, and others, to ensure that they didn't hear the news on the radio. He could face telling the awful news in a way that I couldn't. Cormac's fiancée, Ashlene, had to be informed too and my eldest son, Donal, bravely took on this task.

In the weeks that followed, all our emotions welled-up, but were also kept in check by the endless stream of visitors to our home, including many of the past and present football stars, the managers, and the teams.

I still felt detached and insulated in my grief, and I know that I coped by focusing on the grief of others, particularly Ashlene, whose heart-searing grief tore at my own heart. We talked about everything in the months following his death, particularly Cormac's life, and her five very happy years with him. Ashlene would frequently make the long journey from her home near Derry, and found comfort in being near Cormac's family. We talked about grief, loss and the afterlife. I read everything I could and passed it on to Ashlene. We comforted each other with all the messages of hope we could muster. When she said: "*I know I'll never meet anyone else like Cormac*", I sometimes replied: "*Ashlene, I hope and pray that you will, but, like ourselves, you have only beautiful memories of him, and you had five years of happiness with him. Many couples can be married a lifetime, and not have three months of such happiness.*"

Parents will often say that they never allow themselves to even imagine their child dying, but I had never shied away from the subject of loss and death. In fact, about six weeks before Cormac died, I was walking around the Brantry Lough, where the woods completely surround the water; a place of great beauty and reflection, when I met a very dear friend and we had an interesting conversation. We talked about Cormac's success, and how there was so much activity and even danger in this lifestyle. From this we began to imagine the possibility that something, God forbid, might happen to him or one of the other kids. I now think that I had, in my own way, been preparing for what was to come. I also believe that my own upbringing and early experiences shaped my thinking about fate and death and have given me the courage to get through this difficult time.

From the age of seven or eight, I was very aware of death, and often in a state of terror about many aspects of life and death. Fear was everywhere in those days, with the Bomb, the Cold War, Reds ready to pounce on you everywhere! And in the North, there were echoes of the '56 campaign, and of past executions in Irish history; sectarian tensions reverberated with drumbeats through the air, and hanging still occurred. I instinctively knew the difference between death in the heat of battle, and the cold-bloodedness of the judicial death penalty, which completely horrified me. And after death there was hellfire and demons, or – as it was described - a very boring and insipid heaven – for eternity.

Like others who grew up in the 1960's, I had absorbed much idealistic thought, to the point that I was very anti-war, but still believed that some things were worth fighting for. This and my instincts for self- and family-preservation carried me through "The Troubles". But so many people were just unlucky during those years, struck down at random by a bomb or a bullet. You had to believe in some sort of purpose.

From my need to understand and my continuing curiosity about all aspects of life and death I read books by many modern writers on psychology, philosophy and religion. I have come to believe that death can be a pleasant experience, and that when we die, at our appointed time, we will be going to a place of happiness and rest. Because of this belief I have not, so far, suffered the heart-tearing, the body-convulsing and soul-crunching agonies of grief that so many others do. I have always been aware that death could come suddenly, at random, to anyone. I can only imagine that this is the reason for my calmness and acceptance of what has happened to Cormac and our family.

The past three years have been a totally unpredictable and exhausting time, a whirlwind of public and private activity as so many thousands of people expressed their sympathy, and also their admiration for Cormac, with letters, phone calls, visits, requests for interviews, giving of honours. We have also been asked to attend many social events and to help organise events and fund-raisers.

Within a year of Cormac's death we had set up the Cormac Trust, a charitable trust dedicated to prevention of Sudden Cardiac Death in the young. This work moved ahead very quickly, but also demanded a lot of time and energy from our family. I am still very much involved in this work today.

Brendan, while still grieving deeply, has found focus and consolation in his business and community activities. Donal, who has always been outgoing and expressive, cried copiously after Cormac's death. He has worked very hard for the Trust, taking time out from his studies to meet the many obligations that it brings. All his work over the past three years has taken a toll on his health, but thankfully he is now recovered and he is finishing his post-graduate studies. My son, Fergus, has always been quiet in his grief, and he continues to give solid support to our family. He is coping well, and has found comfort in good friends, hobbies and trips abroad.

Ashlene still grieves but she has found the energy to raise funds for charitable trips to Calcutta and Kilimanjaro, and to keep on playing sport very successfully. These activities have given her focus and the motivation to carry on with her successful teaching career

My journey so far has led me to accept a philosophy of respect and acceptance of the Divine will. I choose to believe that when Cormac died, it was his time, and that he has gone to a place of beauty, to be welcomed by loved ones who have gone before. Rest in Peace, Cormac.

MID-TERM BREAK

This poem was written about ten years after the events it recalls. One thing it does not record is what my father said to me (as the eldest child) on the morning of the funeral. 'Don't be crying. If you cry, they'll all cry.' But I think we all did, anyhow.

I sat all morning in the college sick bay
Counting bells knelling classes to a close.
At two o'clock our neighbours drove me home.

In the porch I met my father crying—
He had always taken funerals in his stride—
And Big Jim Evans saying it was a hard blow.

The baby cooed and laughed and rocked the pram
When I came in, and I was embarrassed
By old men standing up to shake my hand

And tell me they were 'sorry for my trouble',
Whispers informed strangers I was the eldest,
Away at school, as my mother held my hand

In hers and coughed out angry tearless sighs.
At ten o'clock the ambulance arrived
With the corpse, stanched and bandaged by the nurses.

Next morning I went up into the room. Snowdrops
And candles soothed the bedside; I saw him
For the first time in six weeks. Paler now,

Wearing a poppy bruise on his left temple,
He lay in the four foot box as in his cot.
No gaudy scars, the bumper knockect him clear.

A four foot box, a foot for every year.

Reprinted by kind permission of the Poet from *'Death of A Naturalist'*, published by Faber and Faber

MY TWO ANGELS

Our baby daughter, Laura, was born on January 20th 1995 with a hole in her heart. She was a happy, beautiful, little girl; a real Shirley Temple with her mass of curls. She always had a smile on her face, and brought great joy to our house. Laura endured two operations and went on to have a few relatively good years, with the final heart repair operation still to come. Sadly, when it did, on August 31st 1999, Laura did not survive and died, aged just four years. It was such a shock because she was originally expected to come through the surgery and go on to lead a normal life. For my husband, Brendan, and me, Laura's death was a blur: we hardly got to think about it, let alone grieve her at the time, because of what was happening to our other child.

Our daughter, Lynn, who had enjoyed thirteen years of perfect health, was diagnosed with Leukaemia and admitted to hospital. Incredibly this happened on the evening of Laura's final surgery, so we had to cope with Laura's death and Lynn's serious diagnosis within the space of 24 hours. Because of Lynn's condition, we kept Laura in the hospital over night and then took her to our local church the next day and on to Glasnevin cemetery, where she was buried with my parents (she was eventually laid to rest with Lynn at her request and our wish). Lynn had started treatment and as she was quite weak, we were never far from the hospital. We had no choice, we just had to get on with Lynn's treatment and focus on getting her well. Strangely enough, the place in which we spent so much time over the previous four years, now became our home once more, and probably our refuge and support. It seemed almost normal to walk the corridors of Our Lady's Hospital again, but I often wondered if we would ever get out of there.

Lynn lived for almost two more years. She dealt so well with the ups and downs of treatment and when she was in remission for some months, she lived life to the full. At the end, she had a wonderful three weeks in which she knew she was dying, wished it could be different, but accepted it with dignity, all this aged just 15 years. She had great courage and acceptance throughout. Her dying was very open and we had such a lovely time together – peaceful, happy and serene. The closeness of her last week, and her belief that her "angels", (her sister Laura and dear friend, Lorraine who had both pre-deceased her) would be there for her was a great comfort to me – a strange thing to say – but true. She died peacefully at home on the 18th April 2001. Lynn left a list of what she wished friends and family to have, so it was a little easier to give her belongings away. Recently, I felt it was the right time to do the same for Laura. It was much more difficult, as I felt I was almost brushing her away. Laura's clothes have now gone to little girls in Russia and I am still trying to find the right home for her toys. Of course, there are special things belonging to both girls that are very precious and we will never part with them.

How we've coped, five years down the road, is still a bit of a mystery to me. After we married, it was just my husband and I for six years until Lynn came along, and then another nine-year gap before Laura was born. Now, it's just the two of us again and we have to learn to adjust to that. I personally found bereavement counselling a great help. There was nothing in particular that the counsellor said or did that helped, but just having someone on the "outside" to listen was very useful at times.

I also found writing helped with my grief. I wrote to Laura every day after she had died for about a year and since then, I write to both girls on their birthdays, anniversaries, Christmas and other special occasions. I write my own diary every night and always end with words of missing my angels. This helps to keep Lynn and Laura alive for me, although they are not physically here anymore. I have a belief that my two girls are together in a happy place and I draw strength from that.

I notice how differently we cope with our loss. I am very open about everything, and talk, laugh and cry about the girls. My husband is a private person and therefore, deals with the loss in a very different way. Learning to respect the way we each live and cope with our loss can be challenging. However, he is a wonderful support to me and I hope me to him. It is still hard at times to watch friends and family move on with their lives when in some ways time stands still for us – always wondering what might have been.

The awful raw pain of our loss has lessened somewhat, but never fully goes away and never will. We miss Laura's gentle sweetness and Lynn's wonderful sense of fun and enthusiasm for life. I try to remember the good times we had, and that we were fortunate to have our girls – some people are not so lucky. I do believe the old adage: "It's not how long you live, but how you live, that counts". There is no answer to the question 'Why', so I don't ask it too often, as it brings me to a very dark place. I try to live my life now, as I know my girls would wish me to, and I hope one day, to be reunited with them. They are my inspiration.

Setting up of the LauraLynn Charity, to build a children's hospice has become a big focus in my life over the past few years. Having spent so much time with my own children through serious illnesses, I realised there was a lack of respite available to families living with very ill children. The idea was initially sparked by Lynn, whose greatest wish was to die at home, (thankfully that wish was granted to her). The Charity has gone from strength to strength, and the beautiful kind words that often accompany donations help to keep me going. I still get tired and down-hearted at times but I believe the girls will guide me along the way and I feel I owe it to them, to do the best I can. ▣

■ FURTHER INFORMATION ON THE LAURALYNN CHARITY IS AVAILABLE FROM: INFO@LAURALYNNHOSPICE.COM

LYNNS DREAMS

Lynns dreams,

I wish I could learn,
like everyone else,
I wish I could swim, jump & run,
I wish ~~could~~ diffrent cards could have been
dealt,
I wish it could be like old fun.
I wish I could grow & learn about life,
I wish I could feel well again,
I wish ~~there could be~~ that there was an end to the strife,
~~~~ And a new beginning instead.
But destinys come and its drawing me near,
And I know my angels are there,
With them I will have no reason for fear,
In their warm embrace & their care.

By Lynn Mc Kenna
6/4/01

Peter Fallon

ANOTHER ANNIVERSARY

You turn
hearing the joy
of football
in the yard.
You yearn
for that footfall
of the lost,
the scarred.

Again, again
and again
you feel the sten-
gun attack
of that "What if?'
and that 'What then?'
Well, then
he'd be a boy

who's ten.

Reprinted by kind permission of the author and The Gallery Press,
from '*The Company of Horses*' (2007)

BIRTH CRY

My diary tells the story between its blue covers. However, I have been afraid these many years to visit those pages, which confirm the memories.

1976 – a long hot summer- my second baby is due. There are exams in Kings Inns. I am brown as a berry from studying in the garden. On the evening of Sunday 4th July, I am to go to the hospital; the Doctor had recommended a Caesarean section. The room is stark. Nurses come and go. I tell the diary I hope all goes well.

In the morning, there is no pre- med so I did not feel relaxed. A nurse listens to the baby. Everyone agrees this is a big baby. Going into theatre, I see the anaesthetist for the first time. It is a woman. She has heavily made up eyes over her mask, which strikes me as odd. Shivery, I tell her I feel cold. She covers my feet with a blanket. Then the injection…counting into oblivion.

Coming round, I cannot open my eyes. Nobody says anything; I am terribly drowsy, but aware of the muffled silence. In my room now, I see my husband is there. "What is it?"

"A boy, but he is having trouble with his breathing

"Oh God". The anaesthesia draws me back to listlessness.

My mother's face is there. She kept going up to see him in the neo-natal unit. He was very like Portia, his older sister, with black hair, very big, over nine and a half pounds, strong and beautiful.

The quiet tones of the Doctor seated at my bedside. We are taking precautions; it may be his heart or fluid on his lungs. He had given a healthy birth cry; the nurse who had taken him called out "We have lost him Doctor!" We have him in a resuscitator.

I drift in and out of wakefulness not sure what is real what imagined; not sure, what is dream and what is now. I have no sense of time.

Now I am in darkness; there are no voices comforting me with news of how he is.

A rage of thunder rumbles – a shaft of lightening points through the window – a flash ignites the darkness. Torrential rain whips at the window. I am afraid. It is the early hours after 5am. The door bursts open as if by a shudder of the storm – a large black umbrella appears in shadow, my husband is shaking it (I do not remember that umbrella). He walks around to the right of the bed in front of the window.

"What is it? Is he dead?"

We cried a whimpering dry sort of cry. Not yet absorbing the reality. If I close my eyes maybe I will wake to find this was a dream.

After the tempest, I wander inside my head; it is chaos. Two nurses arrive to give me an injection. As they were pulling me up against the back rest, a matron in a dark uniform walks from the door to the left side of the bed, hands me a letter, which read:

"Dear **Mr Quinn**, we regret to inform you that your wife's baby died during the night. Please make funeral arrangements – failure to do so within twenty-four hours will result in the matter being taken in hand by the hospital."

Motionless, I stare at the wall – a wooden crucifix. I am numb. A nurse rushes through the door, blond flicked out hair, looks around officiously and the words ring out "Where's your baby?"

"He died during the night".

She retreats, silenced.

My mother, brother and sisters come, tears dammed back. My husband is involved in funeral arrangements. The Doctor arrives at 4.30. I am arid, stunned, I want an autopsy – some explanation.

My mother divides her time between her granddaughter, Portia and me. What can we say to this four year old who is waiting for the new baby to come home?

The next day my husband brings her into me. Seeing her little expectant face, I weep. My mother takes her off. What would I have done without my mother there? I knew her pain was intense. My father came. He sat on my bed, touched my hand, fumbled for a few words and openly wept. I had never seen him cry.

The Doctor comes. The final analysis was a collapse of the lungs.

The next day, the 8th July was the funeral in Dean's Grange at 9.30. My husband, my brother and two brothers-in-law accompany the little white coffin. My mother came in to be with me and then went to be close to Portia.

I am more aware of things, as if I have just really woken up. It is day four so my breasts swell up and milk comes out. I have never seen my baby. Why did nobody let me see him? Where was he as I lay in this place?

I am feeling sick; I make it to the sink in the corner. I splash my face with water. The effect of the painkillers has now worn off and I am close to the rawness. This has not been a nightmare. I sit slumped and wretched by the sink, the door opens. A tall thin nurse, black turned in hair this time, an angelic face, tensed, reluctant in her task. "Where is your case?" she mumbles.

In her hands, the little nightdress with the ties at the back, the vest and white cardigan that you had to bring in with name tags, are rolled up in a ball and rolling between her nervous fingers.

I point to under the bed. "It is there"

She pulls it out and stuffs this little bundle of his human possessions under my things.

Did he wear these clothes? Did his skin touch these fibres? What was he wearing when he was buried? Nobody ever told me. Dear God, please let this not have happened.

I never held him; he never sensed my touch or my lips on his cheeks, hands or toes. I now long for a sense of his softness and his smell.

I was to hold that little soft bundle close to my chest, in private, over many hours in months to come, and hug them close hoping for some connectedness through which he would be assured of my love- if there were traces of him in these delicate threads – 'heaven's embroidered cloths…'

Tuesday 13th July, a week to the day since Guy's death, I left through the back door of the hospital. Nobody spoke of my baby. All those around me thought it better to avoid the subject and it became a kind of taboo. I yearned for those who saw him to talk of him; to confirm his struggle for life as he tried to breathe.
I cannot bear the thought of my never seeing him; it pierces me sharply still.

We had a bike for Portia to be a present from this new baby on his arrival home. We gave it to her anyway. She appeared wary of the jumbled stories of his being in heaven and how he would have wanted her to have this gift. But you have to say something and you do your best at the time.

Twelve years later in hospital after an operation, I have broken down into uncontrollable tears. I am desperate. I stumble to the bathroom. A nurse knocks on the door, my refuge is secure. "Your tea is cold. I'll get a fresh pot."

Another knock. "Your tea is there getting cold again".

I have to emerge. She is so clever- so good at her job. Through courtesy, not bravery, I make it to the bed choking tears. Not looking directly at me, she says: "I have asked Sr. Maura to come up to you. She is our counsellor".

Dread replaces deep sorrow now – to face some soft, whispery charm – school platitudes or worse... I am vitriolic and I am trapped.

Nothing could be further from the truth of the woman I was to meet.

Sr. Maura appears, makes her way to the chair on my right and asks me about my life. I start to tell her about baby Guy. She talks of some mothers choosing to have a photo of their baby or of holding their baby before putting it into the coffin at funerals to which their family and friends are invited. She discusses the importance of all of this and in so doing calms me. I falter; I try to express my anguish and gripping sadness. I look at her: "Why is this coming to the surface now?"

"You are grieving. You have never grieved this loss".

My daughter was expecting her first baby, in the summer of 2006, when I was trying to write this piece. She is a little older than I was when Guy was born but there are similarities; I try not to reveal my anxiety. We have good times in the summer; walks by the sea and time away together. On 4th September, she goes in to the labour ward about 11am. I am outside trying to be unobtrusive behind the plants in the waiting area.

I speak to my daughter at 1pm and again at 5.30, she is tranquil and happy.

My son arrives at 6.30 soaked from the rain. I have my diary on my lap noting all the events of the day. We wait. I hear a cry at 7.27pm. 'I think that could be...' The chord hovers, it touches something inside me. 'I am sure it is.'

Leo looks doubtfully (there are other babies being born) but with a face that relies on me to know. "Write it down then".

The next 48 minutes were filled with anguish, apprehension and fear. The horror of those days in 1976 engulfed me. It is true; you are never the same again.

At 8.15, we are brought in to see them. Holding the little black haired angel, my daughter smiling, radiant and elated offers her to my arms. She is sucking her fingers. I draw her hand away but meet resistance. She is strong. Child of my child. Thank God.

Months later, she is in my arms; we sway to an African lullaby: 'Thula, thula.' In the darkening light, the street lamp dapples shadows on her face through the window. Blue oval eyes look intently at my face as I hum to the music. There is a profound sense of love in the room. I feel a bond with my angel in heaven who knew no jealousy. He is our witness of hope in the cycle of life. May he watch over his sister and brother, and now little niece, so that all tread softly on their dreams. ▩

Paulyn Marrinan Quinn, Defence Forces Ombudsman, 2006

GRAVE BLANKET

Woolen blanket and marble chippings

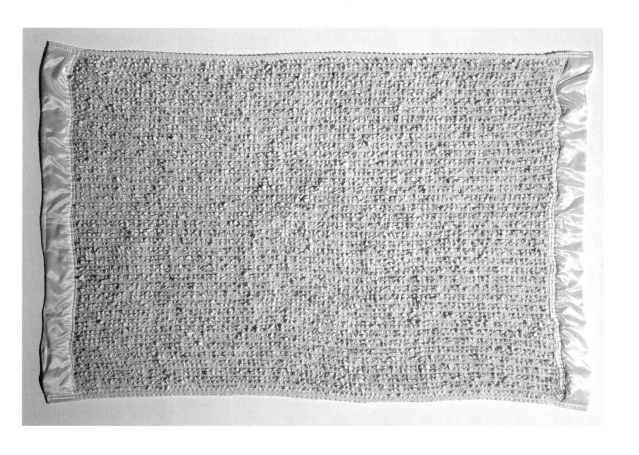

KATHY PRENDERGAST

GRAVE BLANKET (VERSION 1) 1997

THE ONE WHO DIDN'T MAKE IT

I discovered I was pregnant for the second time on my very first Mother's Day. It was unplanned and unwanted, and when the blue line appeared in the window on the pregnancy test, I burst into tears. All on my own in the bathroom, while my husband and our eight-month-old baby daughter plotted an inaugural Mother's Day treat in the kitchen. She had been born two months premature and our shared life so far had been tough. She was still in newborn baby clothes, still on antibiotics and I was still breastfeeding. I was exhausted. The last thing I needed was another pregnancy and another baby.

I dried my tears and went into the kitchen. As soon as I heard the words, 'Happy Mother's Day, 'addressed to me for the very first time, I was off again. In between sobs, I told him I was pregnant. He was as shocked and dismayed as I was. When we'd all calmed down, he said he felt that we were being cheated out of our time with an only child. I just wondered how I'd cope with another baby and I lay awake all that night worrying about it, just me and my unwanted baby.

When did he become wanted? Over the next few days and weeks, while he grew inside me, he somehow found his way into our hearts. Two children under eighteen months started to seem less daunting — even, just possibly, an occasion of joy. We guessed he might be a boy — no reason, just a hunch — and we wondered how he'd get along with his tiny big sister. We told friends and family who slagged us for being nymphomaniacs, who rejoiced with us in anticipation of the chaos ahead. They all told me to take it easy and some advised me to give up breastfeeding. I couldn't do the first and I didn't want to do the second.

At the hospital they performed an early dating scan — the breastfeeding had knocked my menstrual cycle off it's calendar and I'd no idea when I'd conceived. An early dating scan is conducted internally, and is a horrible and invasive procedure — but in the middle of it all, while my dignity was suspended, there he suddenly was on the screen. And there was his tiny heart, beating like a little piston in his barely formed chest. It was a strong and regular beat. And when I saw it, just as I had done when I'd first heard my daughter's heart, I closed my eyes and made a simple prayer; let it still be beating long after my own has stopped.

But it didn't. A week later, going to bed on a Saturday night, something felt wrong. I honestly can't explain what. I wasn't in pain, I had no discharge, but somehow, I knew. The last thing I said to my husband before we went to sleep was 'something's wrong with the baby'. The following morning, I saw that I had bled a little in the night and I knew my baby had died.

At the hospital, though, they weren't so sure. Lots of women bleed slightly in pregnancy, they told me; there really wasn't any reason to fear the worst. Hope surged in my miserable body as they wheeled me to the top floor for another scan. Same drill as before. Only this time, the faces of the technicians told me the result was different. They asked me if I wanted to see him and I said I did. There he was, a tiny thing, a perfect little body lying on his side. And no piston, no heartbeat. He had lived for just ten weeks, which isn't very long. But it was a lifetime.

The next few days are a bit of a blur. Lots of advice, loads of literature, lots of reassurance. Not my fault. Nothing to do with the breastfeeding. Nature's way of dealing with its mistakes. Nobody said anything about my not wanting him in the first place, because by then, I think everyone understood that I wanted him more than anything else in the world. And I still do.

Three days after the scan, I returned to the hospital for a procedure called an Evacuation and Removal of Conception Product. Conception Product. That's what my baby had become. The staff was as sensitive as people who deal with a dozen of these a day can be, but there was a brutality about the whole business, the language, the lack of emotion. All my charts stated that I'd had an 'involuntary abortion a description which seemed to me another kick in my aching abdomen. When I came around from the operation, a wonderful nurse took my hand and asked me how I was. 'Okay,' I muttered through the fading anaesthetic, 'not much pain.' No, 'she repeated, changing the emphasis on her words: 'how are you?' More tears, more pain.

And more questions. Why me? Was it something I'd done? Something I hadn't done? And would it happen again?

And in between the questions, life went on. I minded my baby, kept my house, wrote my jokes. I didn't miss a column deadline. Those who hadn't known about the baby never knew about the miscarriage — in the six years since it happened, this is the first time I've ever mentioned it in public. Well, you don't, do you? And yet, experts estimate that as many as one in four pregnancies end in miscarriage. It is as common as brown-eyed babies, and yet miscarriage remains a taboo subject, a harbinger of awkward silences. You can't be seen to grieve too much, because then you might undermine the pain of parents who've lost children who were born and breathed. It was only ten weeks, after all. Not even a belt notch. Other women don't talk about it, so you too hide it away. Hardly a life, hardly a death. But the grief is real, the bereavement is real and the tears were real. And the guilt — God, the guilt. Was it because we didn't want him enough in the beginning? Was it because our good news seemed like such bad news at the time? Was it the breastfeeding? All you can do is grieve and research. The first helps the heart, the second assuages the guilt. It was nothing we did or didn't do; it could happen to anyone and it does happen to one in three women. We were just unlucky, the research said. But we weren't. We have our health, our lives and three perfect children. It was our tiny, nameless baby who was unlucky.

And life still goes on. Five months after my miscarriage, I was pregnant again. I didn't tell anyone until I was so obviously pregnant that people didn't need to be told. At the hospital they gave out to me for not coming to them sooner, hut I had my reasons. And now I have a big, strapping son who I wouldn't have if I hadn't lost a baby. You can tie yourself up in knots with logic like that, but sometimes it helps. We planted a rose bush in memory of our baby who had no name and no grave, and when we moved back to Dublin, we took it with us and planted it in front of the kitchen window. I'm practical enough to know that the perfect white roses it produces all year round while every other plant in the garden struggles for survival are purely coincidental, but I'm pleased that it thrives.

But it's a rose bush, not a baby. And when I see my three perfect children play around it, I know there should be four of them, that once there were. There are whole days that pass now without me thinking about him, but they aren't many. Most days, I think about who he might have been, this little person who we never met, who we never named, whose gender we never knew. And I remember his heartbeat on a screen, a little piston that stopped short; and it still makes me cry. Because however briefly, I was his mother.

Reproduced with the kind permission of the author, the Sunday Tribune and O' Brien Press, publishers of 'Misadventures in Motherhood' by Fiona Looney, Tanvary 2004

Nuala Ní Dhomhnaill

BREITH ANABAÍ THAR LEAR

Luaimnigh do shíol i mo bhroinn,
d'fháiltios roimh do bhreith.
Dúrt go dtógfainn go cáiréiseach thú
de réir gnása mo nuamhuintire.

An leabhar beannaithe faoi do philiúr
arán is snáthaid i do chliabhán,
léine t'athar anuas ort
is ag do cheann an scuab urláir.

Bhí mo shonas
ag cur thar maoil
go dtí sa deireadh
gur bhris na bainc
is sceith
frog deich seachtainí;
ní mar a shíltear a bhí.

Is anois le teacht na Márta
is an bhreith a bhí
le bhreith i ndán duit
cuireann ribíní bána na taoide
do bhindealáin i gcuimhne dom,
tointe fada na hóinsí.

Is ní raghad
ag féachaint linbh
nuabheirthe mo dhlúthcharad
ar eagla mo shúil mhillteach
do luí air le formad.

Reprinted kind permission of the Poet from *'A Part of Ourselves'*, edited by Siobhán Parkinson
Published by A&A Farmar

Nuala Ní Dhomhnaill

MISCARRIAGE ABROAD

Translated by Michael Hartnett

I had a miscarriage, and about the time the child would have been due I found myself thinking about it. Everyone I spoke to about it said I was mad, and should have got over it by now – hence, 'tointe fada na hóinsí'– even the froth of the sea reminded me of the snagged thread of life which had broken. The poem was a fundamental part of the grieving process.

You, embryo, moved in me—
 I welcomed your emerging
I said I'd rear you carefully
in the manner of my new people-

under your pillow the holy book,
in your cot, bread and a needle:
your father's shirt as an eiderdown
at your head a brush for sweeping.

I was brimming
with happiness
until the dykes broke
and out was swept
a ten-weeks frog—
'the best-laid schemes' . .

And now it's March
your birthday that never was—
and white ribbons of tide
 remind me of baby-clothes,
an imbecile's tangled threads.

And I will not go to see
my best friend's new born child
because of the jealousy
that stares from my evil eye.

Reprinted by kind permission of the Estate of Michael Hartnett c/o The Gallery Press

UNDYING FRIENDSHIP

We think about him every day. A railway bridge straddles our road and the trains wouldn't let us forget him, even if we wanted to. He loved them, knew everything about them, had been there and worn the anorak while never quite turning into one. David Boyd. Irish Railway enthusiast — you called him a train spotter at your peril — extraordinaire. The trains rattle by on their way to Belfast, and we think of him still. I remember the first time I met him. At the railway station in Portadown, on a train to Scarva for the annual outing of the Royal Black Preceptory. My brand-new boyfriend's oldest friend. He made me laugh all the way to Scarva. Me a reporter from the South terrified of saying the wrong thing on a train full of Orangemen; him an irreverent young guy with a wicked sense of humour. He was carrying the banner of the Portadown Orange Lodge, not out of loyalty, but because the 50 quid they paid would make a tiny dent in his student loan. I knew from that first train journey that he was special. That night, Jonny and I were to have our first official date in my hotel. He rang half-an-hour after he was supposed to arrive and asked, "Do you mind if I bring my friend?" Of course I do, you scaredy cat, I thought. "Not at all," I said.

So they arrived. We drank the hotel out of Smirnoff Ice. I started kissing Jonny until he got so embarrassed that he ran away to give Boyd a lift home. On our second date he asked me to go to a party and arrived, late again, to pick me up with Boyd in tow. I almost gave up when Boyd turned up with him a few nights later at the cinema. I soon found out why they seemed joined at the hip during those early days. Jonny's last girlfriend was jealous of their close friendship. He spent less time with Boyd as a result and, when the relationship ended, he felt terrible about the months when he had relegated his snooker pal, his football friend to the second division. A girl was never going to get in the way again. And, despite wanting to be centre of his universe, I was oddly moved by this. Boyd was my text-obsessed mate, my sometimes annoying little brother and the platonic love of my boyfriend's life all rolled into one.

Boyd didn't just know about trains. He had a near photographic memory and a talent for lots of disparate things. One day he wanted to be a journalist, the next a DJ or an international playboy. Once he helped me with an article that involved riding trains all over the six counties. We ended up on the Dublin- bound Enterprise. I wanted to impress him with first-class tickets but you couldn't see well enough from first-class windows for his liking so he dragged me into economy. When we got to my apartment in Dublin, I slept on the sofa and let him sleep in the spare room. He fell out of bed that night. In the morning, dazed and with a bloody nose, he told me he thought this type of thing might have happened before and was perhaps the result of a head injury sustained during part-time work the previous summer. Six months afterwards, he was diagnosed with grand mal epilepsy but neither he nor his parents were warned just how potentially lethal the condition could be.

Jonny's sister made the call to our flat in Belfast late one night when we were just about to go to bed. Is Jonny with you? Something's happened. "What?" it's Boyd. He's dead." I turn to Jonny in panic and I say — what do I say? I take a breath and say, "Jonny, you have to be calm", and he says "What is it?", and starts to cry. He is crying before he even knows And I say, I say, "It's Boyd, he's dead." And that's when my boyfriend collapses like a wet tissue and curls up in a ball on the Boot.

And then we are at Boyd's funeral and it's too real for tears, I can't help wishing the stern-looking minister would say more about who that brilliant boy was in this world instead of telling us to take comfort in the idea that he is on his way to the next. Another victim of sudden unexpected death from epilepsy (SUDEP). Boyd was just 21 when he died from this much misunderstood illness. On our last journey together, I remember looking out at the Coronation Street-style houses with him as the train approached Connolly Station and:, Boyd pointing and saying that is where he would live if he lived in Dublin. We live there now. And it hurts too much to say it out loud, but we miss David Boyd every time the Belfast train goes by. ▨

Reproduced with kind permission of the author and The Irish Times. This article also featured in *'Pieces of Me'*, a collection of the author's work published by Hodder Headline.

Sheila O' Hagan

ELEGY FOR MARK

Mark died three days before his 21st birthday. He loved my daughter and was a constant presence in my house. He was thrown from his motorbike by a drunken driver. He died instantly. In the instant before collision, he positioned his motorbike downwards to save my daughter. I grieve for him as for a son. He left behind a black coat he bought in Oxfam. In the lapel he wore a silver rabbit pin.

In the stored past of an attic
I, a woman growing old,
Hold a coat, Oxfam with rabbit pin
That shapes the lie of your presence,
Arrange the sleeves in an embrace,
Search for a familiar hair, a stain
Mourning as older women do
The bodies of the young.

Watch how your shade invades the pool
Of sun the window has let in,
Hear the purr of the Silver Dream
Racer along a country road,
See it turn treacherous
as you bend to the fatal spin,
The reflection of your stillness
In the still turning wheels.

I, a woman growing old,
Perform a ritual for another's son
Loved as my own, rock myself
Into a grief black as the coat
I hold lest you be there, once a year
Climbing the height of this house
Far from any who might hear
The beat of the heart mending.

Reprinted by kind permission of the Poet from *'A Part of Ourselves'*, edited by Siobhán Parkinson
Published by A&A Famar, 1997

SANCTUARY/WASTELAND

"....Sanctuary/Wasteland refers to Teampall Dumhach Mhor, or 'Church of the Great Sandbank' at Thallabhawn, County Mayo, which lies on the edge of an estuary between Mweelrea Mountain, and the Atlantic Ocean. This site was a monastic settlement from the 6th century and a famine burial ground in the 19th century., Known as 'The Sanctuary' to 17th Century mapmakers, it was referred to as 'The Wastelands' by local people in the 19th and early 20th centuries......"

Irish Museum of Modern Art The Collection, 2005

SANCTUARY/WASTELAND, 1994
DVD PROJECTED INSTALLATION, DIMENSIONS VARIABLE
COLLECTION IRISH MUSEUM OF MODERN ART
PURCHASE, 1997

Brendan Kennelly

BEGIN

Begin again to the summoning birds
to the sight of light at the window,
begin to the roar of morning traffic
all along Pembroke Road.
Every beginning is a promise
born in light and dying in dark
determination and exaltation of springtime
flowering the way to work.
Begin to the pageant of queuing girls
the arrogant loneliness of swans in the canal
bridges linking the past and future
old friends passing though with us still.
Begin to the loneliness that cannot end
since it perhaps is what makes us begin,
begin to wonder at unknown faces
at crying birds in the sudden rain
at branches stark in the willing sunlight
at seagulls foraging for bread
at couples sharing a sunny secret
alone together while making good.
Though we live in a world that dreams of ending
that always seems about to give in
something that will not acknowledge conclusion
insists that we forever begin.

Reprinted by kind permission of the poet from *'Familiar Strangers New and Selected Poems 1960-2004'*
Published by Bloxdale

A NOTE ABOUT THE IRISH HOSPICE FOUNDATION (IHF)

The Irish Hospice Foundation was founded in 1986 and is a not-for-profit organisation that promotes the hospice philosophy and supports the development of hospice and palliative care. Hospice care is the total care of the patient and family at that stage of serious illness when the focus has shifted from treatment aimed at cure, to treatment aimed at facilitating best-possible quality of life. IHF is currently engaged in a range of new projects including; the Hospice Friendly Hospitals programme (a national project to bring hospice principles into hospital practice), the support of children in the community with life-threatening illnesses, and the provision of night-nursing for patients with conditions other than cancer. Approximately 30,000 people die in Ireland each year; the Irish Hospice Foundation's vision is that no one should have to face death without appropriate care and support. This includes support for families as they grieve.

A serious of leaflets about bereavement, and information about bereavement support services are available on our website: www.hospice-foundation.ie

"Irish stories of loss and hope" began as a series of leaflets describing the personal grief experiences of bereavement support volunteers in Dublin hospices. Volunteers provide a much-needed and appreciated listening service to bereaved people.

Design and print | Genprint (Ireland) Limited